Health Ministry

Government Websites

for the

Nations of the World

Paul F. Davis

The nations of the world and their governments are uniquely different, as we learned during the global coronavirus pandemic and their response thereafter. How each nation defines and administers health differs greatly, as do their health policies influencing leadership decisions, regulations, initiatives and guidance for civil society.

This resource is for governments, officials, companies, business and community leaders, concerned citizens and nonprofit organization directors to get connected to the government agencies directing health policy and public health officials serving nations and municipalities therein respectively.

The nations and governments of the world (federal, state and local) are still learning about health, after purporting to know what they were doing during the global pandemic and failing miserably. Of course, few have the humility and decency to admit their failures (lest the corrupt politicians in bed with the pharmaceutical companies not be re-elected).

Among the best and top universities in the world that questioned the necessity of lockdowns and their efficacy to curb, prevent and stop viruses were *Stanford University* and *Johns Hopkins University*. Stanford boldly led the way, a year after which Johns Hopkins sided with the truth and took a stand against the stupidity and widespread human rights violations occurring that eviscerated the United States Constitution and restricted citizens' civil liberties promised therein.

Here below are some articles documenting Stanford and Johns Hopkins scientific studies and findings regarding the ineffectiveness of lockdowns to stop and prevent viruses.

https://siepr.stanford.edu/news/lives-saved-examination-lockdown-policies

https://sites.krieger.jhu.edu/iae/files/2022/01/A-Literature-Review-and-Meta-Analysis-of-the-Effects-of-Lockdowns-on-COVID-19-Mortality.pdf

https://www.aier.org/article/new-study-indicates-lockdowns-didnt-slow-the-spread-of-covid-19/

https://www.washingtonpost.com/dc-md-va/2020/12/16/john-ioannidis-coronavirus-lockdowns-fox-news/

https://padailypost.com/2021/01/18/stanford-study-lockdowns-have-no-clear-benefit/

https://www.dailymail.co.uk/news/article-10321143/We-stop-viral-spread-COVID-end-pandemic-writes-Dr-Jay-Bhattacharya.html

https://health.wusf.usf.edu/health-news-florida/2022-02-02/a-johns-hopkins-study-says-ill-founded-lockdowns-did-little-to-limit-covid-deaths

https://www.medicaleconomics.com/view/john-hopkins-working-paper-says-covid-19-lockdowns-not-worth-it-sparks-fierce-debate

https://www.abcactionnews.com/news/national/coronavirus/johns-hopkins-university-study-finds-lockdowns-only-reduced-covid-deaths-by-0-2

https://padailypost.com/2022/02/07/johns-hopkins-study-finds-lockdowns-didnt-work-should-be-rejected-out-of-hand-in-the-future/

https://thenevadaindependent.com/article/johns-hopkins-study-challenges-the-wild-west-of-lockdowns

https://nypost.com/2022/02/02/covid-lockdowns-had-very-little-effect-on-mortality-rate-study/

https://www.nationalreview.com/corner/johns-hopkins-analysis-lockdowns-should-be-rejected-out-of-hand/

https://www.dailymail.co.uk/news/article-10471265/Johns-Hopkins-professor-blasts-college-media-downplaying-study-COVID-lockdowns.html

   As someone who has earned two Master degrees in Health (University of Alabama) and Global Food Law (Michigan State College of Law) respectively, along with having lived and taught in mainland China for three years; I know a bit about global public health (and the funding of global organizations pretending to serve and advance "health," but rather provide cover for vaccine manufacturers to purport to advise nations and their governments on "health" protocol for optimal wellness, while simultaneously marketing and maximizing the profitability of vaccines worldwide).

I have needed to know about health and wellness as a former lifeguard, personal fitness trainer, and world traveler who has touched 90 nations (having lived in Africa, Asia, Latin America, Europe and North America) in order to survive and sustain myself when living overseas in unfamiliar places.

Some of my books on health, disease prevention and food include:

BREATHE BETTER, HEALTH ADVICE TO IMPROVE BREATHING
~ https://www.amazon.com/dp/1799193160

CONQUERING COVID-19
~ https://tinyurl.com/bye-bye-covid

KILLING CANCER
~ https://www.amazon.com/dp/1096149060

SUBSTANCE ABUSE PREVENTION
~ https://www.amazon.com/dp/1520928521

ALCOHOLISM and DRUNK DRIVING
PREVENTION
~ https://www.amazon.com/dp/1549602721

STOP SMOKING & AIR POLLUTION (fully
illustrated for children)
~ https://www.amazon.com/dp/B0B2HQ3QB
Z

SMOKING PREVENTION - Lessons from
Hawaii
~ https://www.amazon.com/dp/152102748X

EATING AROUND THE WORLD
~ https://www.amazon.com/dp/B0BBY87NX
J

The Future of Food: Global Reform to
Improve the Quality of Food & Public Health
~ https://www.amazon.com/dp/1492173746

The Future of Food: GMOs, Bogus Science,
Agroterrorism and Regulatory Reform
~ https://www.amazon.com/dp/1492174262

GEOSTRATEGY TO PROTECT
ENVIRONMENTAL HEALTH
~ https://www.amazon.com/dp/B00EXVKQF
Q

CHINA'S WATER SECURITY
~ https://www.amazon.com/dp/1520986904

CHINA'S WATER STRUGGLE FOR
SURVIVAL
~ https://www.amazon.com/dp/1520988184

CHILE - ENERGY, ENVIRONMENT & THE
MAPUCHE
~ https://www.amazon.com/dp/B00EXVXT
UK

What I have learned traveling throughout the nations of the world is that everyone defines and approaches health differently. An Australian friend of mine who is married to a Chinese woman with whom he has a child, often told me stories about traditional Chinese health regiments used by grandmothers and mothers with newborns and children to prevent disease and cultivate wellness. Many of these approaches were foreign to my Aussie friend who found some of these health remedies and strategies to be foolish and laughable. Yet, when you consider the Chinese are one of the longest living civilizations; surely they possess some ancient wisdom from which we all can greatly benefit.

Unlike American medical doctors, who usually spend no more than 5 minutes when seeing me (after making me wait in several waiting rooms until they arrive), Chinese acupuncturists usually would spend 45 minutes to an hour asking me questions, learning about my lifestyle, ailments and exploring ways they could treat me naturally with herbs and acupuncture.

As a patient, I have encountered and endured the insensitivity and stupidity of western medicine (often driven by a profit motive and done fast and furiously, while being crippled with a high margin of error and misdiagnoses, up to 25% admittedly by the American Medical Association Journal).

https://jamanetwork.com/journals/jamainternalmedicine/fullarticle/1656540

https://www.ncbi.nlm.nih.gov/pmc/articles/PMC3786666/

Even more frightening is the sad reality that medical errors is the third leading cause of death in the United States. Not surprisingly, American hospitals rarely conduct autopsies on the dead to cover their tracks, hide their negligence, avoid documenting or calling attention to medical errors, and save themselves money in court from medical malpractice and legal liability.

https://www.cnbc.com/2018/02/22/medical-errors-third-leading-cause-of-death-in-america.html

https://hub.jhu.edu/2016/05/03/medical-errors-third-leading-cause-of-death/

https://www.jdsupra.com/legalnews/medical-error-ranks-as-no-3-killer-in-u-15309/

https://pubmed.ncbi.nlm.nih.gov/28186008/

https://www.jstor.org/stable/j.ctt18z4gww

https://www.washingtonpost.com/news/to-your-health/wp/2016/05/03/researchers-medical-errors-now-third-leading-cause-of-death-in-united-states/

"A wise man will hear, and will increase learning; and a man of understanding shall attain unto wise counsels" (Proverbs 1:5).

"Give instruction to a wise man, and he will be yet wiser: teach a just man, and he will increase in learning" (Proverbs 9:9).

"The wise in heart shall be called prudent: and the sweetness of the lips increase learning" (Proverbs 16:21).

"The heart of the wise teaches his mouth, and adds learning to his lips" (Proverbs 16:23).

"Give attendance to reading, to exhortation, to doctrine" (1Timothy 4:13).

Paul F. Davis is a wellness trainer, worldwide inspirational speaker, international educator (licensed in Florida and California) and UCLA certified University and Career Counselor serving students and professionals. Paul speaks for governments, companies, schools, colleges and universities throughout the world on a number of topics including:
- Peak Performance
- Disease Prevention
- Living with Purity and Purpose
- Happiness and Success
- Discipline and Sacrifice
- Commitment, Consecration and Courage
- Living Your Dreams
- Substance Abuse Prevention

PaulFDavis.com
EducationPro.us
Tinyurl.com/PaulFDavis-Books

RevivingNations@yahoo.com

Hereafter are 42 pages
with the names of government ministries of
health throughout the nations of the world
with the accompanying websites
to easily access.

Ministry of Health Government Websites

Afghanistan Ministry of Health

https://moph.gov.af/

Albania Ministry of Health

https://shendetesia.gov.al/

Algeria Ministry of Health

https://www.aps.dz/en/health-science-technology/tag/Ministry%20of%20Health,%20Population%20and%20Hospital%20Reform

Andorra Ministry of Health

https://www.salut.ad/

Angola Ministry of Health

https://minsa.gov.ao/ao/

Antigua and Barbuda Ministry of Health

https://health.gov.ag/

Argentina Ministry of Health

https://www.argentina.gob.ar/salud

Armenia Ministry of Health

https://www.moh.am/#1/0

Australia Ministry of Health

https://www.health.gov.au/

Austria Ministry of Health

https://www.sozialministerium.at/en.html

Azerbaijan Ministry of Health

https://www.sehiyye.gov.az/en/

Baden Ministry of Health

https://sozialministerium.baden-wuerttemberg.de/de/startseite

Bahamas Ministry of Health

https://www.bahamas.gov.bs/health

Bahrain Ministry of Health

https://www.moh.gov.bh/?lang=en

Bangladesh Ministry of Health

http://www.mohfw.gov.bd/

Barbados Ministry of Health

https://www.gov.bb/ministries/health

Bavaria Ministry of Health

https://www.bundesregierung.de/breg-en/federal-government/ministries/federal-ministry-of-health

Belarus Ministry of Health

http://minzdrav.gov.by/en/

Belgium Federal Ministry of Health

https://www.health.belgium.be/en

Belize Ministry of Health

https://www.health.gov.bz/

Benin Ministry of Health

https://sante.gouv.bj/

Bolivia Ministry of Health

https://www.minsalud.gob.bo/

Bosnia and Herzegovina Ministry of Health

https://fbihvlada.gov.ba/

Botswana Ministry of Health

https://www.moh.gov.bw/

Brazil Ministry of Health

https://www.gov.br/anvisa/pt-br/english

Brunei Ministry of Health

https://www.moh.gov.bn/Pages/Home.aspx

Bulgaria Ministry of Health

https://www.mh.government.bg/en/

Burma Ministry of Health

www.mohs.gov.mm

Burundi Ministry of Health

http://minisante.bi/

Cabo Verde Ministry of Health

https://minsaude.gov.cv/

Cambodia Ministry of Health

http://moh.gov.kh/?lang=en

Cameroon Ministry of Health

https://www.minsante.cm/site/?q=en

Canada Ministry of Health

https://www.canada.ca/en/health-canada.html

Cayman Islands Ministry of Health

https://www.gov.ky/health-wellness/home

Central African Ministry of Health

https://wwwnc.cdc.gov/travel/destinations/traveler/none/central-african-republic

Chad Ministry of Health

https://socialprotection.org/connect/stakeholders/chad-minist%C3%A8re-de-la-sant%C3%A9-publique-ministry-health

Chile Ministry of Health

https://www.gob.cl/en/ministries/ministry-of-health/

China Ministry of Health

http://en.nhc.gov.cn/

Colombia Ministry of Health

https://www.minsalud.gov.co/English/Pagina
s/Minister.aspx

Comoros Ministry of Health

https://beit-salam.km/les-
pr%C3%A9sidents/

Costa Rica Ministry of Health

https://www.ministeriodesalud.go.cr/

Cote d'Ivoire (Ivory Coast) Ministry of Health

https://guce.gouv.ci/sante?lang=en_US

Croatia Ministry of Health

https://zdravlje.gov.hr/

Cuba Ministry of Health

https://salud.msp.gob.cu/language/en/welco
me-to-the-official-website-of-the-ministry-of-
public-health/

Cyprus Ministries Health

https://www.moh.gov.cy/moh/moh.nsf/index
_en/index_en

Czech Republic Ministry of Health

https://www.mzcr.cz/en/the-ministry-of-
health/

Democratic Republic of Congo

Ministry of Health

https://www.minisanterdc.cd/

Denmark Health Ministry

https://sum.dk/english

Djibouti Ministry of Health

https://sante.gouv.dj/

Dominica Ministry of Health

http://health.gov.dm/

Dominican Republic Ministry of Health

https://www.msp.gob.do/web/

Ecuador Ministry of Health

https://www.salud.gob.ec/coronavirus-covid-19/

Egypt Ministry of Health

https://healthcode.mohp.gov.eg/gc/

El Salvador Ministry of Health

https://www.salud.gob.sv/

Equatorial Guinea Ministry of Health

https://guineasalud.org/

Estonia Ministry of Health

https://www.sm.ee/

https://e-estonia.com/solutions/healthcare/e-health-records/

Eswatini Ministry of Health

https://www.gov.sz/index.php?option=com_content&view=article&id=267&Itemid=403

Ethiopia Ministry of Health

https://www.moh.gov.et/site/

Fiji Ministry of Health:

https://www.health.gov.fj/

Finland Ministry of Health

https://stm.fi/en/frontpage

France Ministry of Health

https://sante.gouv.fr/spip.php

Gabon Ministry of Health

https://www.sante.gouv.ga/

Gambia Ministry of Health:

https://www.moh.gov.gm/

Georgia Ministry of Health

https://www.moh.gov.ge/

Germany Ministry of Health

https://www.bundesgesundheitsministerium.de/

Ghana Ministry of Health

https://www.moh.gov.gh/

Greece Ministry of Health

https://www.moh.gov.gr/

Grenada Ministry of Health

http://www.gov.gd/index.php/health

Guatemala Ministry of Health

https://www.mspas.gob.gt/

Guinea Ministry of Health

http://sante.gov.gn/

Guinea-Bissau Ministry of Health

https://web.facebook.com/minsapgw/?_rdc=1&_rdr

http://www.guinebissaurepublic.com/health-2/

Guyana Ministry of Health

http://www.health.gov.gy/

Haiti Ministry of Health

https://www.mspp.gouv.ht/

Holy See (Vatican) Ministry of Health

https://www.vatican.va/content/vatican/en.html

Honduras Ministry of Health

https://www.salud.gob.hn/

Hungary Ministry of Health

https://kormany.hu/emberi-eroforrasok-miniszteriuma

Iceland Ministry of Health

https://www.government.is/ministries/ministry-of-health/

India Ministry of Health

https://mohfw.gov.in/

Indonesia Ministry of Health

https://www.kemkes.go.id/

Iran Ministry of Health

https://behdasht.gov.ir/

Iraq Ministry of Health

https://moh.gov.iq/

Ireland Ministry of Health

https://www.gov.ie/en/organisation/department-of-health/

Israel Ministry of Health

https://www.gov.il/he/departments/ministry_of_health/govil-landing-page

Italy Ministry of Health

https://www.salute.gov.it/portale/home.html

Jamaica Ministry of Health

https://www.moh.gov.jm/

Japan Ministry of Health

https://www.mhlw.go.jp/english/

Jordan Ministry of Health

http://www.moh.gov.jo/

Kazakhstan Ministry of Health

https://www.gov.kz/memleket/entities/dsm?lang=en

Kenya Ministry of Health

https://www.health.go.ke/

Kingdom of Serbia/Yugoslavia Ministry of Health

https://www.zdravlje.gov.rs/

Kiribati Ministry of Health

https://mhms.gov.ki/

Korea Ministry of Health

https://www.mohw.go.kr/eng/

Kosovo Ministry of Health

https://msh.rks-gov.net/en/

Kuwait Ministry of Health

https://www.moh.gov.kw/en/Pages/default.aspx

Kyrgyzstan Ministry of Health

http://www.med.kg/en/

Laos Ministry of Health

https://moh.gov.la/

Latvia Ministry of Health

https://www.vm.gov.lv/lv

Lebanon Ministry of Health

https://www.moph.gov.lb/

Lesotho Ministry of Health

https://www.gov.ls/ministry-of-health-to-make-agreement-with-vaccine-producer/

Liberia Ministry of Health

http://moh.gov.lr/

Libya Ministry of Health

http://health-ministry.ly/

Liechtenstein Ministry of Health

https://www.liechtenstein.li/en

Lithuania Ministry of Health

https://sam.lrv.lt/

Luxembourg Ministry of Health

https://msan.gouvernement.lu/fr.html

Madagascar Ministry of Health

http://www.sante.gov.mg/

Malawi Ministry of Health

http://www.health.gov.mw/

Malaysia Ministry of Health

https://www.moh.gov.my/

Maldives Ministry of Health

https://health.gov.mv/dv

Mali Ministry of Health

http://www.sante.gov.ml/

Malta Ministry of Health

https://deputyprimeminister.gov.mt/en/Pages/health.aspx

Marshall Islands Ministry of Health

https://rmihealth.org/

Mauritania Ministry of Health

https://www.sante.gov.mr/

Mauritius Ministry of Health

https://health.govmu.org/Pages/default.aspx

Mexico Ministry of Health

https://www.gob.mx/salud

Micronesia Ministry of Health

https://hsa.gov.fm/

Monaco Ministry of Health

https://www.gouv.mc/Gouvernement-et-Institutions/Le-Gouvernement/Departement-des-Affaires-Sociales-et-de-la-Sante

Mongolia Ministry of Health

https://moh.gov.mn/

Montenegro Ministry of Health

https://www.gov.me/mzd

Morocco Ministry of Health

https://www.sante.gov.ma/Pages/Accueil.asp
x

Mozambique Ministry of Health

https://www.misau.gov.mz/

Myanmar Ministry of Health

www.mohs.gov.mm

Namibia Ministry of Health

https://mhss.gov.na/

Nauru Ministry of Health

http://www.naurugov.nr/government/ministr
ies.aspx

Nepal Ministry of Health

https://mohp.gov.np/np

Netherlands Ministry of Health

https://www.government.nl/ministries/minis
try-of-health-welfare-and-sport

New Zealand Ministry of Health

https://www.health.govt.nz/

Nicaragua Ministry of Health

http://www.minsa.gob.ni/

Niger Ministry of Health

https://www.sante.gouvne.org/

Nigeria Ministry of Health

https://www.health.gov.ng/

North Macedonia Ministry of Health

http://zdravstvo.gov.mk/

North Korea Ministry of Health

http://www.moph.gov.kp/en/

Norway Ministry of Health

https://www.regjeringen.no/en/dep/ho
d/id421/

Oman Ministry of Health

https://www.moh.gov.om/ar/1

Pakistan Ministry of Health

https://nhsrc.gov.pk/

Palau Ministry of Health

http://www.palauhealth.org/

Palestine Ministry of Health

https://www.moh.gov.ps/portal/

Papua New Guinea Ministry of Health

https://www.health.gov.pg/

Panama Ministry of Health

https://www.minsa.gob.pa/

Peru Ministry of Health

https://www.gob.pe/minsa/

Philippines Ministry of Health

https://doh.gov.ph/

Poland Ministry of Health

https://www.gov.pl/web/zdrowie

Portugal Ministry of Health

https://www.dgs.pt/

Qatar Ministry of Health

https://www.moph.gov.qa/arabic/Pages/default.aspx

Republic of Korea (South Korea) Ministry of Health

http://www.mohw.go.kr/eng/

Romania Ministry of Health

https://www.ms.ro/

Russia Ministry of Health

https://minzdrav.gov.ru/

Rwanda Ministry of Health

https://www.moh.gov.rw/

Saint Lucia Ministry of Health

https://health.govt.lc/

Saint Vincent and the Grenadines
Ministry of Health

http://www.health.gov.vc/health/

Samoa Ministry of Health

http://www.samoagovt.ws/tag/ministry
-of-health/

San Marino Ministry of Health

https://www.sanita.sm/

Sao Tome and Principe
Ministry of Health

https://ms.gov.st/

Saudi Arabia Ministry of Health

https://www.moh.gov.sa/Pages/Default.aspx

Senegal Ministry of Health

https://sante.sec.gouv.sn/

Serbia Ministry of Health

https://www.zdravlje.gov.rs/

Seychelles Ministry of Health

https://www.gov.sc/GovernmentAgenci
es/Ministry/minhealth.aspx

Sierra Leone Ministry of Health

https://mohs.gov.sl/

Singapore Ministry of Health

https://www.moh.gov.sg/

Slovakia Ministry of Health

https://www.health.gov.sk/Titulka

Slovenia Ministry of Health

https://www.gov.si/en/state-
authorities/ministries/ministry-of-health/

Solomon Islands Ministry of Health

https://solomons.gov.sb/ministry-of-health-medical-services/

Somalia Ministry of Health

http://moh.gov.so/en/

South Africa Ministry of Health

https://www.health.gov.za/

Spain Ministry of Health

https://www.sanidad.gob.es/

Sri Lanka Ministry of Health

http://www.health.gov.lk/

Sudan Ministry of Health

http://www.fmoh.gov.sd/

Suriname Ministry of Health

http://health.gov.sr/

Sweden Ministry of Health

https://www.government.se/government-of-sweden/ministry-of-health-and-social-affairs/

Switzerland Ministry of Health

https://www.bag.admin.ch/bag/en/home.html

Syria Ministry of Health

http://www.moh.gov.sy/

Tajikistan Ministry of Health

https://adbmch.tj/

Tanzania Ministry of Health

https://www.moh.go.tz/index.php

Thailand Ministry of Health

https://www.moph.go.th/

Timor-Leste Ministry of Health

http://www.ms.gov.tl/en

Togo Ministry of Health

https://sante.gouv.tg/

Tonga Ministry of Health

http://www.health.gov.to/

Trinidad and Tobago

Ministry of Health

https://health.gov.tt/

Tunisia Ministry of Health

http://www.santetunisie.rns.tn/fr/

Turkey Ministry of Health

https://www.saglik.gov.tr/

Turkmenistan Ministry of Health

https://skyscraperpage.com/cities/?buildingID=55044

Uganda Ministry of Health

https://www.health.go.ug/

Ukraine Ministry of Health

https://en.moz.gov.ua/

United Arab Emirates Ministry of Health

https://mohap.gov.ae/en/Pages/default.aspx

United Kingdom Ministry of Health

https://www.gov.uk/government/organisations/department-of-health-and-social-care

USA Ministry of Health

https://www.hhs.gov/

Center for Disease Control and Prevention

https://www.cdc.gov/

United States Department of Agriculture

https://www.usda.gov/

U.S. Food and Drug Administration

https://www.fda.gov/

U.S. Department of Health and Human Services

https://www.healthcare.gov/

U.S. Department of Health Care Services

https://www.dhcs.ca.gov/

Uruguay Ministry of Health

https://www.gub.uy/ministerio-salud-publica/home

Uzbekistan Ministry of Health

https://ssv.uz/

Vanuatu Ministry of Health

https://moh.gov.vu/

Venezuela Ministry of Health

http://mpps.gob.ve/

Vietnam Ministry of Health

https://moh.gov.vn/

Yemen Ministry of Health

https://moh.gov.ye/

Zambia Ministry of Health

https://www.moh.gov.zm/

Zimbabwe Ministry of Health

http://www.mohcc.gov.zw/

Global Health Data Exchange

https://ghdx.healthdata.org/

Thank you for reading this book. If you know of any other government health websites you would like to add to this book, you are welcome to email Paul and suggest they be added.

If you would like to hire Paul to research a particular aspect of the global public health, a specific country, region, economy, industry, provide a report and/or evaluation on the viability of a health policy and/or proposal; please email Paul to discuss the matter further.

Paul F. Davis is a wellness trainer, global business consultant, worldwide inspirational speaker, international educator (licensed in Florida and California) and UCLA certified University and Career Counselor. Paul speaks for governments, companies and universities worldwide on a number of topics.

PaulFDavis.com
EducationPro.us
Tinyurl.com/PaulFDavis-Books
RevivingNations@yahoo/com

Please email Paul to check his availability to speak in your city and/or provide consulting services.

www.ingramcontent.com/pod-product-compliance
Lightning Source LLC
Chambersburg PA
CBHW070837220526
45466CB00002B/800